Dance in the Church: What's the Pointe?

Other Books By The Author

Processionals, Props, & Pageantry
Dancing for Him
Dance, Dance, Dance!
Team Terrificus
Creative Worship
Divine Choreography
Prophetic Dance

Dance in the Church: What's the Pointe?

Practical Answers to
Reasonable Questions for
Pastors, Dancers, & Congregations

SECOND EDITION 2006

Book Design: Jessica Mitchem

Production: SPS Publications Eustis, Florida

www.spsbooks.com

Dedication

To my good friend and mentor, Linda Jones, who initiated the thought process for this book by asking me the question, "What *is* the point?"

Contents

INTRODUCTION

A few years ago, my husband and I were visiting our friend in New Orleans. We were discussing, at that time, my first book *Dancing For Him*. We poured over every detail with great delight. Somehow, we got to the place in our evaluation and critique where she said (somewhat jokingly): "so, what *is* the point?" Without ever answering or exploring it, we simply smiled, shrugged our shoulders, and walked away. I did, however, ponder that question all the way home. In fact, during that long car ride, I heard the voice of the Lord say, "write a book called *Dance In The Church, What's The Point.*" He immediately, proceeded to give me ideas and inspirations.

Since dance has, in the past, carried with it some negative connotations, the idea of having it in our churches bucks against many people's beliefs and philosophies. There are many questions that are raised in the minds and hearts of Pastors, dancers, and congregations.

My goal and purpose in this book, is to take a look at some of those probing, reasonable questions and try to answer them, practically, with God's guidance. Hopefully, this book, in the hands of inquiring minds and skeptical hearts, will help alleviate doubt and judgment. Pondering Pastors will have a better understanding about their sheep, who are called to dance for the Lord, and not be as concerned about what the rest of their congregation will think or do in response to them. Dancers, who have this unique calling to dance for our King, and who often find themselves in a dilemma, will gain better understanding of their call, as we explore some heartfelt questions. Finally, critiquing congregations and the population at large, will less likely *point* a finger toward those who are *pointing* their toes, as we all explore…"What's the *Pointe*?"

ONE

PASTORS PONDER

Questions

- *If I consider dance as a viable ministry in my church and let some dance, won't I run the risk of losing some of my other parishioners?*

- *Where in the Bible does it mention waving a flag over someone?*

- *The traditional Easter drama has always been fine by itself. Why should we include dance?*

II Chronicles 5:13-14

13 *"Indeed it came to pass, when the trum-
peters and singers were as one, to make one
sound to be heard in praising and thanking
the Lord, and when they lifted up their voice
with the trumpets and cymbals and instru-
ments of music, and praised the Lord, say-
ing: "For He is good, For His mercy endures
forever," that the house, the house of the Lord,
was filled with a cloud,*

14 *so that the priests could not continue min-
istering because of the cloud; for the glory of
the Lord filled the house of God."*[2]

Thanking—*Yadah —"to hold out or use the hand, to revere or worship with extended,* flourishing *hands"*[2]

Flourishing—*"to make showy, wavy motions, as of the arms; anything done in a showy way, as a sweeping movement of the limbs or body; a waving in the air; brandishing"*[1]

At the writing of this book, my husband and I have only very recently become pastors of a local church. The premises on which we base our foundation and by which we present the gospel message are the Word of God and the arts. Therefore, I can not comfort a pastor, who has never seen the arts (particularly dance) in the church, from personal "pastoral" experience. I can not base my counsel on an evolutionary process, as a pastor who once did not embrace the dance and now allows it occasionally in the service, because our services started, therein, entrenched.

I can only offer encouragement, comfort, hope, and education based on my many years as a minister of dance. In my travels, I have worked very closely with pastors, from many different denominations, all over the country and abroad. I have listened attentively, heard their pastoral hearts, and tucked their concerns deep in my heart. Now, is the time to release the information that will help pastors, dancers, and congregations know what the point of having dance in the church is.

Three major reasons, the Lord has shown me, for having dance in the church are: demonstrative praise and worship, warfare, and winning souls. The three questions that were raised by pastors, in the beginning of this chapter, coincide or parallel these three *points* respectively.

This book is not intended to be an exhaustive biblical study or dissertation about the subject. I have several other books that disclose, in great depth, the Hebrew and Greek words and definitions for dance. I encourage you to read them to acquire even greater knowledge. However, as we take a look at these questions, I do desire to offer hope and comfort, along with a general understanding, about the point of dance in the church.

Q **If I consider dance as a viable ministry in my church and let some dance, won't I run the risk of losing some of my other parishioners?**

To put it bluntly and answer abruptly, yes. That is probably not what you wanted to hear. However, it is the truth. Even if you explained the dance from the pulpit every Sunday, had fliers in the back, and offered extra classes on the subject, there will still be those to whom it is repulsive. Hence, you would lose them. The question then becomes, are you, the pastor, willing to risk losing some of your parishioners for the sake of allowing dance in your church? Please read on.

I know that initially, this does not offer much comfort. However, when you have a better understanding of why it may be worth the risk, you will become more at ease.

Let's take a closer look at the scripture in the beginning of this chapter. This is one of my favorite because it gives such a vivid illustration of unity, movement, and God's presence. In this scripture (2 Chron. 5:12-14), we see how many people were in unity during their praise and worship. We also see that when they were praising and *thanking* God, during that time of unity, they were participating in much movement (dance is movement). We learned that the word "thanking" (yadah) means (for reiteration): to hold out or use the hand, to revere or worship with extended, *flourishing* hands"[2] and *flourishing* means "to make showy, wavy motions, as of the arms; anything done in a showy way, as a sweeping movement of the limbs or body; a waving in the air; brandishing."[1] They were all in one accord and they were *moving* (perhaps in unity). It was after this unified activity of music and dancing that the glory of the Lord fell.

Wouldn't it stand to reason, then, that if we were to follow this scriptural example, that the Glory of God's presence would fall, in our churches, in such a powerful way that the ministers would not even be able to stand? What happens when the presence of God is evident? In His presence is fullness of joy (Ps. 16:11). Being in His presence is being surrounded with songs of deliverance (Ps. 32:7). There is also healing of all kinds of diseases, just to name a few.

Herein lies a paradoxical problem and another question to ponder. If dance is allowed in the church and some people stay, observe and are in disagreement with it, then there can be no complete unity, hence, the presence of God may not show up in a powerful manifestation. If dance is not allowed in the church, and there are no unified movements of praise (like the scriptural example), the presence of God may, also, not show up in a powerful manifestation.

Conversely, however, if dance and unified movements of praise and worship are active in the church and those who were in disagreement with it leave, then there will be a much greater chance for the presence of God to show up in a powerful manifestation. The question to ponder then becomes, do we want to hang on to our people (who we as pastors love so dearly) or do we hunger after God and want His presence manifested in our services so much that we are willing to let them go?

Q: Where in the Bible does it mention waving a flag over someone?

As I said earlier, the three points that the Lord wanted me to bring up were basically, worship, warfare, and winning souls. Since I answered the first question by relating it to praise and worship, then this question will relate to warfare.

On an elementary level, we understand that we do not battle against flesh and blood but against principalities, powers, etc. In the heavenly places (spiritual warfare) (Eph. 6:12). There are no *specific* instances in the Bible where someone waved a flag over someone (the way we envision it today). There are several examples, however, of the use of banners or flags that signify various meanings. When we understand what flags (or banners) represent and combine that knowledge with the understanding of certain types of movements and colors, then we have a whole arsenal of spiritual references with which to do battle.

I strongly recommend reading my other books that go into great detail about this subject. The Processionals, Props, and Pageantry book, especially, cites many examples. For your convenience, and for greater understanding, I will insert a small sample. There are so many references in the Word about flags (or banners). However, to best explain them in this context, the following examples, definitions, and scriptural references, prove to be the most appropriate.

Before I go into those examples and scriptures to verify the validity of flag waving as warfare, I would first like to share a testimony from one of our meetings. In brief, there were two lines of people. The front line was ready to receive from the Lord. The back line was ready to minister to them by waving flags over their heads. The music began and they commenced waving. At first, it seemed as if nothing was happening. Then, suddenly, we could literally feel the presence of God in a powerful way. Some of the people in the front line began crying, some began to shake, some fell to their knees, and some went through deliverance. How does one explain something like that? The only way I know is with the following definitions and scriptures.

Wave Offering—Tnuwphah (ten-oo-faw)—*A perfume of fire that drives out the occupant (enemy). Similarly, sweet incense to God (Nicowach) means restful delight.–A brandishing (threat); by implication, tumult; specifically the official undulation of sacrificial offerings—offering, shaking, wave (offering).*[3]

Root word—nuwph (noof)—*a primitive root; to quiver (i.e. vibrate up and down, or rock to and fro); lift up, move, offer, perfume, send, shake, sift, strike, wave.*[3]

When we praise the Lord by waving our hands (with or without a flag or banner) we can activate peace and rest in our lives because we are literally driving out the enemy of our soul (doing warfare). Since it is his job to steal, kill, and destroy anything that is, has, or gives life, then it is our job to foil those plans with the foe-defeating power of the Holy Spirit. Giving birth to Spirit-inspired dances and implement-handled movements is a catalyst that can execute a sweet smelling 'savor wave' that drives out the occupant, causing deliverance. The remaining fruit is salvation, life, rest, and peace to the demonstrative "praiser", and in many cases, the quiescent on-looker.

Isaiah 59:19—*"So shall they fear the name of the Lord form the West, and His glory from the rising of the sun. When the enemy comes in like a flood, the Spirit of the Lord will lift up a standard against him."*[2]

We are certain that the enemy of our soul will come into close contact with the invincible and overpowering Spirit of the Living God. A presentation of a banner can literally cause the enemy to flee because the Spirit of the Lord is the one who lifts up a standard against him. It invades the air space of the prince of the power of the air, and destroys him.

This insight along with an understanding that the colors of the banners are significant, will prove to wreak havoc in the enemy's camp! Again, the Processional book goes into great detail. However, here is a very small sample of what some colors represent.

Red—*blood of Jesus, war, consuming fire*

Gold—*glory of God*

Green—*healing, life, prosperity*

Purple—*majesty*

In summary, if a worshipper in your church were to pick up a green flag and wave it over someone, the following is what it could signify: Since green represents healing and a waving motion drives away the enemy of our souls, then a manifestation of healing could occur in the individual under which the banner is being waved! The example combinations are endless, but you get the *point*.

Q: The traditional Easter drama has always been fine by itself. Why should we include dance?

This comment/question came from a pastor in a very traditional and strict denomination. Every year their church put on fabulously elaborate (and costly) drama productions. People from other churches would often come and visit, just to enjoy them. They had never seen dance in the church, so when one of their parishioners (who was instrumental in putting together the dramas) asked if she could include or introduce dance, you can only imagine their response. In essence, their mental questioning was, dance in the church, what's the point? This challenging question began that woman's mission to get dance in her church. She began to communicate more frequently and openly by sharing the scriptures that she had learned, with her pastor and music minister. Her music minister even attended one of my Dancing for Him Worship Dance Workshops. The leadership of her church really had a hunger to know the truth about dance in the church and when they discovered it, they embraced it. They allowed this woman to not only include it in the big Easter presentation, but also let her do specials during some of their church services. This very conservative church went so far as to allow dancing during their worship services (although it was met with some resistance by the more traditional members). What was the key? Education. Once they familiarized themselves with the scriptural foundations on which dance is based, they were much more willing to accept it.

There are literally hundreds of scriptures (366 to be exact) that allude to or speak about some type of movement (dance is movement). To avoid being redundant, I am going to refer you to my Dance, Dance, Dance! book which references these. To get you started, though, there are a few references with in this book.

The question was why dance, when drama, alone seems successful and complete. The answer, in addition to all the scriptures that back dance, is about winning souls.

Sometimes, when a person who is lost or backslidden, does manage to make it to a church, they kind of know what to expect. If they didn't experience it when they were children, they may have seen it on television, or heard about it by word of mouth. They know they will probably hear some kind of music (choir, band, organ, hymns, etc.). They can also expect to receive some kind of preaching. Because this is normal and expected, a rebellious heart could possibly turn a deaf ear to even the best expository. A drama usually touches hearts by the mere fact that it is dramatic. Even this, however, if it is an Easter or Christmas presentation, can be mundane to the yawning, heart hardened intellectual. Don't get me wrong. Music, in conjunction with life changing messages and dramas have been instrumental in bringing countless thousands to salvation. I'm proving, here, the validity of dance (not discounting the other methods of soul winning). I'm also talking about those lost souls with cynical, unsentimental hearts that have been tough to crack by other means. This type of person whose mind is seared and whose heart is case-hardened, will sometimes turn a deaf ear to the expected. However, when this soul is bombarded with a whole arsenal of spiritual weaponry found in an anointed dance, the winning of their soul may become easier. Their senses will be touched in several ways. They will hear the music, see movement, hear the words of the song, see the interpretation, and possibly even feel the anointing. Because this type of tactic can often slip past the mental barrier of resistance (by-pass the mind) and go directly to the heart, victory over the enemy in their mind, will, and emotions, can more easily be obtained. They can then be won to God's side! Hence, soul winning.

Worship, warfare, and winning souls are all very good *points* to prove why some should point*e* their toes while others should not *point* their fingers.

TWO

DANCER'S DILEMMA

QUESTIONS

- *Praise Him with the dance—Yeah, but now?*
- *Do I just want to perform for acceptance?*
- *If do not "out do" the last performance, or I do a bad dance, does it mean that it will not be anointed or will not minister?*

John 4:23

23 *"But the hour is coming, and now is, when the true worshipers will worship the Father in spirit and truth; for the Father is seeking such to worship Him."*[2]

Worship—*Proskuneo*—*"to prostrate oneself in homage; to kiss the Master's hand."*[2] *It is a physical demonstration of total, intimate, spiritual abandonment, which shows sacrificial love to the Lord. This is done through movement of going from a standing position to lying down in humble prostration.*

As one who has worshipped, through movement, for the Lord since 1986 (you do the math), I have often found myself in a mental dilemma with regard to dance in the church. With out coming right out and saying the words "what's the point?" I have, over the years, inadvertently asked myself that question. It did not take long to find proof that dance was scriptural. The predicament was more in the honest discovery of my own motivation.

In one of the better dance team practice times that I attended, the question was raised: "Why do you dance (in church, of course)." Each person in the room had to come up with an answer. The majority of the team was comprised of teenagers, who, much to my surprise, offered honest comments that were heartfelt and spiritual. Some struggled with their reply because, quite frankly, they had never really thought about it. Some of the answers (mostly from adults) were well spoken. However, it was as if we were digging for 'the right thing to say' (so as not to look badly or 'loose face'). If we dive deeply to examine our hearts and ask ourselves this question, what kind of answers surface?

Each of the questions in the beginning of this chapter, I have either asked myself or heard others pose. Let's take a look at each of them.

Q: Praise Him with the dance—Yeah, but *now?*

I don't know how many times, over the years, I struggled with this question. After that prompting by the Holy Spirit, during a worship service, it seemed like I would constantly give myself *at least* a forty second counseling session. Before moving out to dance, I would have seemingly endless battles and conversations going on in my mind.

First, I would check to see if it was really the Lord who wanted me to dance or was it me... Lord...me...Lord...me...Lord...me. When I concluded that, in fact, it was the Lord, then the battle was about what the people would think. Would I distract them from worship or draw them in...distract...draw...distract... draw...distract...draw. Then I would remember the scripture in Proverbs 29:25 that says: "The fear of man brings a snare, But whoever trusts in the Lord shall be safe."[2] Ok, so I remembered I was safe. Then came more battles. What was my motivation? Did I want to be seen as a good dancer with talent, did I want exposure, or was I a true worshipper who *worshipped* the Father in spirit and truth? Did I give a physical demonstration of total, spiritual abandonment? It seemed that the enemy wanted me to believe that I wanted to be seen so he could fulfill his purpose which was to kill the inspiration, steal the anointing, and destroy any hope of someone being healed through the dance. Once I realized that—*yes*, it was God who wanted me to dance, and *yes*, I would be drawing the people into a higher realm of worship through my total, intimate, spiritual abandonment, (which showed sacrificial love to the Lord) and *yes*, God did not give me a spirit of fear, but of love, power and a sound mind, then, like a horse at a released starting gate, I bolted to obedience.

The results were always astounding to me. People would come up afterward and tell me that they were so glad I danced, for various reasons. Some would say that they always wanted to dance but, for one reason or another, were unable. My obedience gave them a visual outlet to not only dance in the physical, but also would draw them into a higher realm of worship. They thanked me. Others, would tell me that they experienced a powerful anointing and went through deliverance when I danced. I don't fully understand the spiritual ramifications, but one can not argue with a testimony. Still others were glad that I moved out in the dance because it gave them strength or courage to move up to the next level in their own form of worship movement. It set them free to be able to express their love to the Lord more demonstratively.

I might add here, that I was blessed to be in a church where the Pastor gave me total liberty and authority, as the dance leader, to move out into the aisle or front area when I felt lead by the Spirit of God. I encourage you, if you are going to follow my testimonial example, that you first check with your covering to make sure they are in agreement with your passion and call. Make sure you have permission from your spiritual authority to dance in church and find out from them, what the acceptable boundaries are.

Q: Do I just want to perform for acceptance?

This is the type of question that you immediately respond by saying, "of course not!" Honestly speaking, however, let us again examine our hearts.

I have been dancing since 1966 (you do the math). During at least ten of those years, I was in an annual recital. As a teen, I was involved in other performances as well. As a young adult, I was in two different college dance companies and finally in a professional ballet company. Along with performances come applause, accolades, congratulations for a job well done, audience appeal, and mass acceptance. For anyone who has even a hint of low self-esteem, is motivated by praise, or has fear of rejection, performance is seemingly the answer behind which to hide.

We don't like to use the word performance in our presentation dances. But in reality, there is an element of performance by mere virtue of doing something in front of people who watch the dance with their eyes open!

Let's take an honest look again at our heart motivation and address this issue. Especially for those of us who have been performers for any length of time, this becomes an internal struggle. Although it is often not consciously on the surface, it is still there.

Throughout our Christian walk, we discover things about ourselves that we ask

God to help us root out. I know I suffered from low self-esteem and fear of rejection. I also felt like if I wasn't producing something (performing a task or dance for acceptance), that my personal value was questionable. Therefore, when I would put together presentations in the church, that were received with thunderous applause, subconsciously, it would make me feel like I had self-worth. Of course, I would never admit to this false belief, mostly because I either didn't realize it or was in denial. If I had realized it, I certainly wouldn't have wanted people to think anything less of me then what was holy and acceptable. Because of this unconscious denial, I truly believed that I always did the presentations for God's glory. In innocence, I'm sure I was covered, but there is a continual process of dying to self and letting Him take full control of our lives.

However, when I confessed the false belief (that I was accepted for what I did and not for who I was in Christ) as sin and came to the realization that I am totally and fully accepted in the Beloved (who is all that matters anyway), I was set free to truly dance for Him! This freedom helped me to know, with confidence, that the presentations He gave to me were for His purposes and not mine.

Know that you are not just tolerated by God. You can never be more acceptable to Him than you are at this moment. "For He made Him who knew no sin to be sin for us, that we might become the righteousness of God in Him (2 Cor.5:21)."[2] You are not what others think of you, which feeds the lie about fear of rejection, nor acceptable to God because of your merit. You are, however, fully pleasing, and completely acceptable to God, only because of Christ (Rom. 5:8-10). Therefore, the point of presentations should not be for our acceptance from the Lord or the people, but to demonstrate *His* Word for *His* glory.

Q: If I do not "out do" the last performance, or I do a bad dance, does it mean that it will not be anointed or will not minister?

Let's go back to the words in the title of the book. What is the point of dance in the church? Have we overlooked the importance of the presence and anointing of God in our dances? Have we fallen away from doing dances that minister to Him and the viewers? If so, we need to re-examine our purpose and motive.

Sometimes, especially if we've been in the dance ministry for a while and the dances have been highly anointed, we may get the impression that we have to 'out do' the last dance with a better one. We may think, how can we top that last one? I know those thoughts have run through my mind on occasion. For example, when we use props (cloths, streamers, banners, etc.) to visually magnify the message, we may be tempted to get bigger, better, and fancier cloths. Maybe we need more flags, more tambourines, more props. Maybe we should use faster, more up-beat songs. Gee wiz, let's swing from the chandeliers and shoot fire from cannons in the back! The people would like that. Who are we trying to please anyway?

With all joking aside, we need to focus all our attention on the Lord. We need to be at His feet, in His presence, and receiving divine revelatory dances from Him alone. All the wonderful ideas of man, pyrotechnics, and computerized light shows in the world pale bleakly to the power and magnificence of His glory that radiates, resplendently, from a Spirit-inspired dance. We do not have to 'out do' the last dance. We should not be the ones in control anyway. If we have been in His presence and are doing the dance that He wants when He wants it done, then the result will be ministry. We, who are called to the dance ministry, are to be ministers first and then dancers. I am sure you have heard it said that it is more difficult to teach a dancer to minister then it is to teach a minister to dance.

What is a 'bad' dance anyway? Is it a dance done without any skill? By whose standards do we constitute the formula for a 'bad' dance? If someone has no training, has a heart of worship, and has a desire to minister to the Lord with total abandon, should they be allowed to dance before the congregation or be on the team? You bet! Are the dances they do anointed? I have seen dances over the years, done by people who had virtually no training, that literally moved the audience to tears. I saw a mime/dance combination one time that I'll never forget. The anointing was so strong, that you could literally feel it all the way in the back of the huge auditorium. Those ladies obviously had very little technical experience but that didn't stop the move of God through the hearts of men. It seems to be that a true worshippers pure heart is what makes a significant difference. This is not to say that we should throw all training to the wind. Or discount a spirit of excellence. By all means, improving skill is beneficial.

One of the points of dance in the church is not to see if we can out do each other or the last dance we did. It is not to discourage the inexperienced dancer or to disallow less then perfection. However, if we who are true worshippers, humbly come before the Lord and seek His will for the dance that He wants presented in this day and hour, then, in this case, the point of dance in the church, is to bring forth His anointing. This will break the yoke of bondage, ministering life and healing to the onlooker. If His formula for success and direction for destiny is followed, no one will expect a greater performance or better dance.

The battle in the mind may be about obedience, fear of rejection, or out doing your last performance. However, He rewards those who diligently seek Him. You are accepted in the Beloved, and no one ever has to (nor can they) out do His performance. So what's the point? *Worship* the Lord in spirit and in truth.

THREE

CONGREGATIONAL CRITIQUE

QUESTIONS

- *Did David perform for the people or did he minister to God?*

- *"Aren't those dancers just drawing attention to themselves and distracting the congregation from worship?"*

- *"I liked everything about the service until she did that dance. Does dance really belong in a church service?"*

II Samuel 6:14-16

14 *"Then David danced before the Lord with all his might; and David was wearing a linen ephod.*

15 *So David and all the house of Israel brought up the ark of the Lord with shouting and with the sound of the trumpet.*

16 *Now as the ark of the Lord came into the City of David, Michal, Saul's daughter, looked through a window and saw King David leaping and whirling before the Lord; and she despised him in her heart."*[1]

Danced—*Karar*—*"comes from the root word (Kar) which means battering ram, and Karar means to whirl."*[3] *Therefore, this type of dance could mean: a battering ram that whirls against the enemy!*

Whether you are a Pastor, an elder, or a leader of some kind, you were at one time or another part of a congregation. We've all been or still are an audience of sorts. As a church service takes place, we all make some kind of (at least) mental notes or judgments. How many times have we gone home from church and verbally rated the worship service, or had "roast Pastor" for lunch? "I'd give the worship about a six today—last Sunday was definitely an eight!" No one wants to admit it, but we have probably all done it at one time or another and it needs to be addressed. It is often not until you are in a place or seat of authority that you truly understand what the leadership goes through.

Because dance in the church is quite controversial anyway, it often receives the brunt of ridicule, judgment, and pointing fingers. Again, all of the questions in the front of this chapter, I have either heard people say or pondered myself. My purpose, here, is not so much to educate or prove dance scripturally (many of my other books do that thoroughly-please avail yourself to the resources in the back of this book), as it is to explore the thoughts and intents or our hearts. This chapter will hopefully comfort worship dancers by honest, relatable sharing and expose the other side to congregations so we may do less critical critiques.

Q: Did David perform for the people or did he minister to God?

As we look at the opening scripture in this chapter, we notice that David danced before the Lord with all his might. Was he performing for the people? It seems not. Reflecting on the beginning of chapter six (in II Samuel), we discover that David's heart was always toward God. He honored the presence of God. He had respect for the Lord by not doing anything with the ark for three months. He was repentant when he realized that they didn't carry the ark the way they were supposed to, after which, he rectified the situation (which showed integrity). He also had a giving heart as he blessed the people with food. He obviously displayed a heart after God, with good, godly character, and did not care as much about what the people thought as his wife did. She only mocked him as she thought he shamelessly uncovered himself. His heart was to please God and minister to Him. Without re-addressing the issue of performing for acceptance, let's look at it for its own sake and hold it up against ministry.

Many years ago, I attended a dance conference where I picked up a flier labeled, "Performing?/Ministering?" I have since then tried to find out who the author is, but to no avail. I would like to print it for the benefit of you the reader and hope that if you are the author of this great quote, that you will forgive me for printing it without footnoting your reference. It is quite good and bears repetition.

It seems as though David aspired to minister to God and in doing so, inadvertently, ministered to the people. He obviously did not care about performing for the people. He was almost oblivious to them (during his time of abandoned worship).

Why is it, in some of our churches today, that dance is not accepted. Christmas and Easter drama performances are universally accepted and promoted. Choir performances are hailed, praised, and expected. In each of these cases, the talents of actors and singers are used and applauded. What's wrong with the talent of a dancer? Dramas and cantatas are acceptably able to present the gospel message in an alternative (other then preaching) form. Who says dance can not? Is it because dance is not spoken or sung? Is it because the dancers themselves do not speak or sing? What about the words of the song to which they are dancing, does that not proclaim the message of the King? OK, then what is the point of dance in the church? If we compare it to drama, which is often speaking about the gospel message, or cantatas, which are singing about the gospel message, then we have to look at the fact that a dance done to music with words has three elements. A dance has music in the background, words done to melody in the foreground, and has movements to interpret the words for tremendous impact! We have compared apples to apples with regard to certain forms of acceptable performance in the church. Now, however, let's compare those apples to oranges.

If we went to watch the New York City Ballet perform *Swan Lake,* would we leave the theatre and say: "What a powerful anointing; I really sensed the power of God; I have been healed and my life has been changed forever?" Of course not. More then likely, we would exclaim what a wonderful performance it was. The ballet company works tirelessly to please the people in the audience. Herein lies the difference. A good performer is concerned about what people think. A good performance evokes a response of applause. A dance minister, on the other hand, is more concerned about what is on God's mind. Also, rather then looking for an immediate *response* from the people, they should hear about the life changing *results* of ministry. In this case, the point of dance in the church should not be that it is just on the same plane as drama or choir and should be let in based on its similar performance merit. If that were the case, dance could easily be accepted once it is understood. It is also not to say that dance is better in any way then drama or cantatas or that dramas or cantatas do not minister. The issue here is dance. Therefore, because it is classified or considered ministry, that, in and of itself, may very well be the main reason that it is not accepted. Just like Michal did not like

David's ministry unto God because it went against the system of the king. Could it be that dance as ministry goes against the religious systems (or religious spirits) of our world today? Something to think about.

Q: Aren't those dancers just drawing attention to themselves and distracting the congregation from worship?

David's heart was to minister to God. Michal's heart was to criticize and judge. When David took off his kingly robe and danced in front of the people in his ephod, that was an insult to Michal. She was totally embarrassed by her husbands actions. Not only was he celebrating among the common people, but he also took off his robe which represented a breaking of the traditions of the king. David showed his boldness against the traditions of men and abandon to the Lord by proclaiming that he will be even more undignified before the Lord and he will be held in honor. (vs. 22)

Michal is referred to in this scripture as Saul's daughter (representing the lineage of royalty) as opposed to being referred to as David's wife. So, she was taking sides, as it were, for what she thought was "better" and observed her husband's behavior as going against that which was "acceptable." She was sitting in the seat of judgment while her husband was worshipping. One person's actions were the type that would have been more pleasing in the sight of a king or worldly rulers. However, one's actions were more pleasing in the sight of God. One was pointing a judgmental finger of accusation, while one was pointing all the attention and focus toward God. Which one was doing the better thing, the finger pointing critical judge (Michal) or the one who was worshipping God with his whole heart (David)?

If there are dancers in the church that are worshipping with their whole hearts (like David did) and on the other hand, there are others in the congregation who are just stewing because of it (like Michal), which ones are doing the better thing? *Ouch*. Are the dancers just trying to draw attention to themselves? Are they really trying to distract the congregation from worship? As you read in chapter two, if a dancer is truly called to minister, there is usually a great inner struggle about whether to dance or NOT dance so as NOT to draw attention to themselves or to distract.

Upon closer observation, let's look at the heart of the person in the congregation and why they would pose a question like the one mentioned earlier. If, while in the congregation (during worship), we are so caught up in God's presence and basking in the anointing (with our eyes only on Him), then how is it even possible to focus our attention on the dancer (unless, we purposely watch and allow him or her to draw us in to a higher realm of worship)? How is there even potential to be distracted by someone else who is also worshipping (through dance), if we are enraptured in God's glory?

Look at the result of Michal's criticism. She was unfruitful (had no children) to the day of her death. (vs. 23) Does this mean that if we stand in judgment or criticize, that we will be barren or unfruitful? It may not literally mean we will have no children. However, it is a point about worth asking the Lord and about worth thinking before we raise a critical finger of judgment. We should, rather follow the example of David and worship with our whole being, which is an appropriate response to our Lord's presence.

Q: I liked everything about the service until she did that dance. Does dance really belong in a church service?

One time, Tom and I ministered at a very small denominational church in New England. How did a prophetic dance ministry that flows in healing, personal prophesy and dance get in there? Only God knows! He showed Himself powerfully, throughout all the revival services, though.

To digress momentarily, I have to share this testimony. At the end of the first service (where there was worship, dancing, and a message), we encouraged the people to come forward to receive prayer for healing. There was that seemingly endless moment of silence, as if time stood still. No one moved. They weren't used to this. Finally, one brave soul came forward. This frail, petite woman must have been at least eighty-five years young. All eyes were on her as she made her way to the front of the church. The only sound in the room was the clicking of her heels on the two hundred year old wooden floor.

Once at the front, she trustingly placed herself before us to receive a faith-filled prayer. Perhaps everyone else was thinking, "if she gets healed, maybe I'll go up." I smiled and very appropriately and ever-so-gently laid one hand on her shoulder. I then barely touched her forehead with a finger from my other hand. No sooner did I utter the words, "Lord, thank you for this precious vessel of honor..." when suddenly: BANG! It sounded like a gun shot went off. The next thing I knew, this delicate woman had hit her head on the wood pew on her way to the floor.

Tom said that the rest of the people in the congregation gasped, held on to the pews in front of them, and slowly peered over to see if she was still alive. The power of the Holy Ghost hit her in a mighty way (which was unfamiliar to many in attendance). I quickly scooped her up in my arms and asked if she was alright, to which she replied, "that's the second time that's happened to me." She kind of giggled and went back to her seat. My first thought was, "oh no, everyone is going to leave." But, surprisingly, many more people came forward for prayer. What a powerful service it turned out to be. Glory to God!

After it was all said and done, and people were finally going home, one gentleman remained and talked with Tom. He made the statement, "I liked everything about the service until she did that dance. Does dance really belong in a church service?"

With much wisdom, my husband's reply was not that which would produce a doctrine battle (because it was obvious this man knew scripture). He simply said, "my wife was raised in a good home, in a good neighborhood, is well educated, and has been trained for some thirty years in dance. The thing is, she became a Christian. With all her years of training in dance, and because she is not a singer or (at the time) an orator, does she have no place in the church? Let me ask you this: what would *you* do with her?" Those questions seemed to stop him right in his tracks. He smiled, and thoughtfully pondered.

What *do* we do with someone who is skilled in an area that we are not used to seeing in the church? Because someone dances instead of sings or does mime instead of preach, do we shun them or diminish their value in the body of Christ? Certainly not!

Obviously, there should be certain standards of dress, Christian music, an attitude of reverence, and a minister's heart evident before a dancer presents a piece. However, with all that in place, and the scriptural knowledge of its validity, what holds us back from acceptance? Perhaps it is tradition. Perhaps it has just never been done before. Perhaps we inherently do not like change. What ever the reason, we need to ask the Lord what *He* would say about the matter. Ask Him what is the point of having dance in the church. Ask *Him* what we should do with a dancer. Sometimes, an anointed dance will by-pass the mind and penetrate even the hardest of sinners' hearts with a "moving" message of salvation.

Sometimes, it is a lack of understanding. Sometimes it is a critical spirit. Sometimes it is just personal taste. What ever it is, that stops one from believing that dance should be in church, needs to be examined. Once a person knows the dance minister's heart, understands that they do not want to draw attention to themselves, and can look past their own likes or dislikes, then the point of dance in the church becomes more clear. It can be seen as ministry unto God and man. It can be seen as a viable means through which the gospel message may be presented and it can serve as a unique method by which salvation and healing is facilitated.

Conclusion

So...what is the point of having dance in the church? To a pastor, who may be concerned about losing his sheep, it may mean making an important sacrifice in order to house God's presence. To a dancer, who loves to perform, it may mean taking a closer look at their motivation in order to gain freedom for themselves and others. To people in the congregation, who may have been spiritual score keepers, it may mean examining the temptation to have critical thoughts toward others. So, the point is not just about how pretty dancers look when they point their toes. The issues go much deeper. By allowing dance in our churches, God may *point His* finger toward our hearts...

Bibliography

[1] *Webster's New World Dictionary of the American Language*
All definitions throughout
Simon and Schuster, a division of Gulf and Western Corp. ©1982
1230 Avenue of the Americas
New York, New York 10020

[2] *Spirit Filled Life Bible – New King James Version*
All scriptures throughout and some comments
Thomas Nelson Publishers – Nashville
Atlanta – London – Vancouver
Thomas Nelson, Inc. ©1991
General Editor – Jack W. Hayford, Litt. D.
Old Testament Editor – Sam Middlebrook, D. Min.
New Testament Editor – Jerry Horner, Th.D.
Assistant Editor – Gary Mastdorf, M.S.

[3] *The Exhaustive Concordance of the Bible*
Abingdon Press, Nashville Forty-second Printing 1983
James Strong Madison, N.J.
Key Word Comparison © 1980 by Abingdon

About the Author

As an ordained minister of the gospel of Jesus Christ, Lynn and her husband travel extensively and visually demonstrate the Word. She is a well-known author and producer of eight books, one calendar, and over 19 videos/dvd's about worship dance. As founder of DFH, Lynn (with over 40 years of dance experience behind her) has dedicated all her ballet, modern, jazz, and choreography technique to the Lord for His glory. She performed with the Towson State University dance company, and the Ballet Theatre of Annapolis; assisted the choreographer and danced in Integrity Hosanna's music video "Sing Out" with Ron Kenoly; and was on the teaching staff at Christian International's Arts Conferences for several years. She orchestrates worship dance workshops and conferences literally around the world. During these Spirit inspired events, there is an activation and impartation of an unparalleled style of prophetic worship dance. She is a leader of leaders. Many people that she has mentored over the years now have their own dance teams and some of them hold workshops, themselves. There is a unique ability to lead large groups and congregations in corporate worship dance and presentations. She also ministers in dance directly to the congregation with an anointing that breaks the yoke of bondage, heals and delivers!

FOR FURTHER INFORMATION ABOUT:

- Attending one of our conferences
- Having us minister at your church
- Hosting a workshop in your area
- Getting on our mailing list
- Ordering more resources

Please feel free to contact us at:

(800)787-1623
info@dancingforhim.com
www.dancingforhim.com